American Patriotic Symbols

Author	Linda Milliken
Illustrator	Barb Lorseyedi

EP075 ©Lab Safety Supply Inc. 1996, 2002, 2007
401 S. Wright Rd.
Janesville, WI 53547

Table of Contents

The Hands-on Heritage series has been designed to help you bring culture to life in your classroom! Look for the "For the Teacher" headings to find information to help you prepare for activities. Simply block out these sections when reproducing pages for student use.

Patriotism

The word patriotism means "love of country." People with patriotic feelings have a sense of belonging to their country and support its beliefs, customs, and institutions. Patriotism usually means attachment to the land and the people, as well as devotion to the welfare of the community.

People often display and express their patriotism through the use of patriotic symbols. Many poems and songs have been written to express the strong ties between people and their nation. Symbols such as national flags, statues, and buildings often remind people of their country's history. People all over the world celebrate their patriotism with national holidays and parades.

Project
Complete a word search that contains terms relating to patriotism.

Materials
- pencil

Directions
Find and circle the words in the Patriotic Word Search.

For the Teacher
Copy one Patriotic Word Search (below) per student.

Patriotic Word Search

Abraham Lincoln

American Flag

Anthem

Capitol

Eagle

Great Seal

Liberty Bell

National

Parade

President

Stars

Stripes

Uncle Sam

Washington

A	R	N	A	T	I	O	N	A	L	M	Y	W	L
N	M	T	R	E	W	Q	O	U	I	G	L	A	C
T	Y	E	P	U	I	O	P	L	B	K	A	S	L
H	C	X	R	Z	D	F	G	H	E	J	E	H	O
E	V	B	E	I	S	E	P	I	R	T	S	I	T
M	U	I	S	O	C	I	O	P	T	A	T	N	I
E	T	R	I	E	W	A	D	F	Y	G	A	G	P
A	K	A	D	P	J	R	N	M	B	H	E	T	A
G	S	M	E	Z	L	K	J	F	E	A	R	O	C
L	R	A	N	G	B	O	Q	G	L	E	G	N	R
E	A	G	T	S	I	N	A	E	L	A	V	L	S
F	T	E	E	D	A	R	A	P	L	Q	G	O	B
H	S	T	D	A	M	A	S	E	L	C	N	U	G
N	L	O	C	N	I	L	M	A	H	A	R	B	A

The National Flag

Probably the most important patriotic symbol is the national flag, which represents the land, people, and government of the United States.

The Continental Congress determined on June 14, 1777, that the "Flag of the United States be 13 stripes, alternate red and white; and the Union be 13 stars, white in a blue field, representing a new constellation." Since Congress did not mandate how the stars should be arranged, flag makers offered various designs.

Over the years, various presidents decided on new arrangements for the stars when a new state entered the Union. Sometimes new designs were worked out by the army and navy. Presidential orders determined how the stars would be positioned for 48 stars in 1912, and again in 1960 for 50 stars.

Project

Form cooperative groups to create paper flags that illustrate changes in the national flag over the last 200+ years. Complete some fun flag projects on page 6.

Materials

- Flag Cards
- red, white, and blue butcher paper
- ruler or other measuring tool
- scissors
- glue
- Star Patterns

Directions

1. Divide into eight cooperative groups.
2. Use the following color key when making your flag:

Red    **Blue**

3. Follow the flag illustration on the card to recreate a paper flag. Assign tasks among group members: measure, sketch, cut, and glue. Determine the finished size of the flag before beginning.
4. When the flags are complete, compare the similarities and differences. Create a display for the school entry, office, or cafeteria.

For the Teacher

Copy and cut apart the Flag Cards (page 5) and give one card to each group. Copy one Star Patterns (page 9) per student and one National Flag Projects (page 6) and assign for each student.

    EP075 American Patriotic Symbols © Lab Safety Supply Inc. 2007

The National Flag Cards

Continental Colors
America's first national flag, 1775–1777

Flag of 1777
By Congressional Resolution, 1777–1795

Flag of 1777
Rarely used circle design, 1777

Flag of 1795
15 stars and stripes for 15 states, 1795

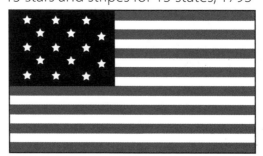

Flag of 1818
13 stripes and a star for each state, 1818

Great Star Flag
Used occasionally, 1818

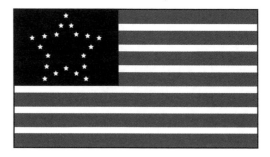

48-Star Flag
Served longer than any other, 1912–1959

50-Star Flag
The current flag, 1960–present

National Flag Projects

Here are some fun ways to recreate the National Flag!

Paper-chain Flag

Materials

- red, white, and blue construction paper
- Star Patterns
- scissors
- glue
- ruler
- pencil

Directions

1. Measure and cut paper into 2 x 5-inch (5 x 12.7-cm) strips.
2. Create paper chains with the strips. Make each chain all the same color or create patterns.
3. Assemble the chains in rows on the classroom wall to create the national flag. Staple the chains in place at several points. Cut stars to glue on.

Box-top Flag

Materials

- rectangular-shaped gift box
- red, white, blue tissue paper
- scissors
- starch
- ruler
- pencil

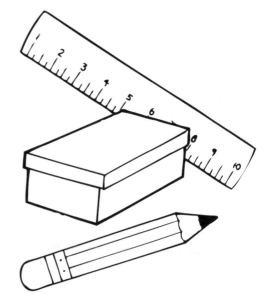

Directions

1. Measure and mark lines on the box top to duplicate the national flag.
2. Cut tissue paper into the necessary shapes to create the flag. Brush each piece in place on the box top with starch slightly diluted with water.
3. Allow the lid to dry completely. Use the box as desktop storage.

Bunting

During a campaign or presidential speech, political party convention, or other patriotic event, the national flag has a prominent place on a speaker's platform, but is never used for decoration. You will see, instead, the speaker's platform or the wall behind the speaker draped in red, white, and blue cloth. This decorative draping is called bunting. Bunting should be arranged with blue at the top, white in the center, and red at the bottom.

Bunting is also the term used for the woolen cloth used in making flags.

Project

Make bunting to drape and decorate the classroom walls. This project should be done outside on a grassy area.

Materials

- old white sheets or cloth
- clothespins
- red and blue dye
- masking tape
- disposable plastic gloves
- fabric scissors
- clothesline or rope
- large buckets or tubs

Directions

1. Cut the sheets or cloth in strips about 12 inches (30.48 cm) wide.
2. Follow the directions on the packages to make batches of red and blue dye in several buckets. Leave some buckets empty for transporting dyed cloth strips and for rinsing.
3. One group dyes the cloth strips. Another rinses the strips. A third hangs them to dry.
4. Together, drape the dry cloth strips on the wall, blue on top, white in the middle, and red on the bottom. Hold the cloth in place with masking tape or pins.

For the Teacher

Assign students into work groups, each having a different responsibility in the dyeing process. All participating students should wear plastic gloves.

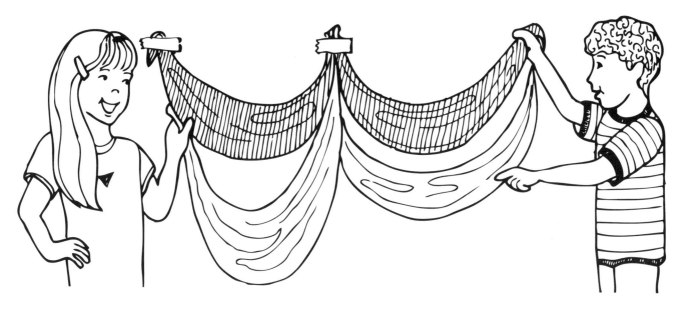

Stars and Stripes

"Stars and Stripes" is a popular name for the national flag of the United States. No one knows when this expression was first used to refer to the flag, but these two shapes have become synonymous with American patriotism. They are used as decoration on campaign posters and buttons, decorative bunting, and patriotic banners.

The five-pointed star and red and blue stripes symbolize the union of the states. They represent the land, the people, the government of the United States, and the ideals upon which the country was founded.

Project
Make a Stars and Stripes T-shirt.

Materials
- white, red, or blue T-shirt
- cardboard
- scissors
- red, white, and blue fabric paint
- Star Patterns

Directions
1. On a piece of paper, sketch a design of stars and stripes that you'd like to apply to your T-shirt.

2. When you are happy with your design, make star stamps by tracing the Star Patterns onto cardboard and cutting them out. Then make long rectangular stamps out of cardboard.

3. Using different colored fabric paint, stamp your design on your T-shirt. Wear it to show your patriotism!

For the Teacher
Copy one Star Patterns (page 9) per student.

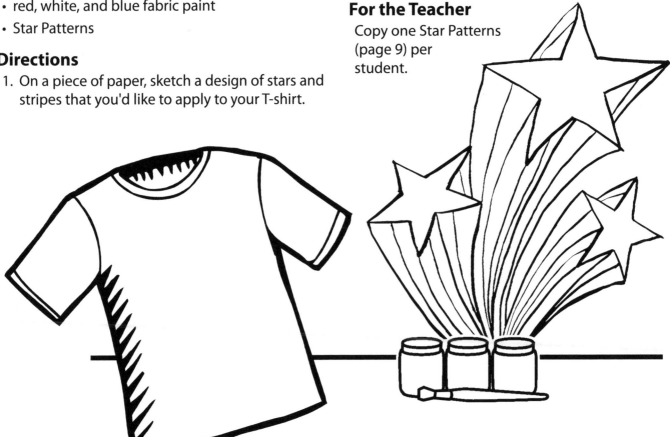

 EP075 American Patriotic Symbols © Lab Safety Supply Inc. 2007

Star Patterns

Red, White, and Blue

Red, white, and blue are the three colors that have come to symbolize American patriotism.

The Continental Congress did not indicate why it chose red, white, and blue as the colors for the American flag. However, the Congress of the Confederation chose these same colors for the Great Seal of the United States in 1782. The meaning for each of the colors was stated in the resolution on the seal.

Red—for hardiness and courage.

White—for purity and innocence.

Blue—for vigilance, perseverance, and justice.

Project
Choose one of the Patriotic Decorations projects to dress up the classroom in patriotic colors. The materials you will need appear in bold type.

Patriotic Twirler

Start with **red, white, or blue tagboard circles.** Have your teacher poke a hole in the middle. Draw a spiral extending from the hole to the edge of the lid. Use a **scissors** to carefully cut, following the line. Use glue to draw a design on your twirler, then sprinkle silver or gold **glitter** on the design. Let it dry. Tie **red, white, or blue yarn** to the middle of the spiral to hang from the ceiling.

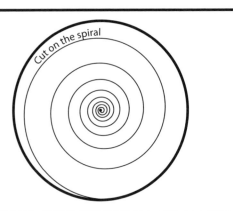

Patriotic Garland

Cut patriotic shapes from **red, white, and blue construction paper**. Use a **hole-punch** to make a hole at the top of each shape. Use **string** to tie the shapes on **thick yarn** to create a garland to drape across the classroom walls or ceiling.

Red, White, and Blue Projects

Crepe-Paper Windsock

Cut a **poster board** strip and **staple** the ends together to form a circle. Use **scissors** to cut and **tape** strips of alternating **red, white, and blue crepe paper** to the inside of the circle. Staple another poster board strip to the circle to create a handle. Hang from the ceiling.

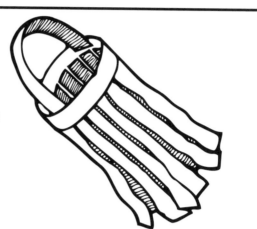

Ribbon Rally

Using three **small paper dessert plates**, draw a "U" on one, an "S" on another, and an "A" on the third. Decorate the plates with **red, white, and blue curling ribbon, satin ribbon, trims, and bows. Glue** the plates side-by-side on **tag board** for a U.S.A. banner.

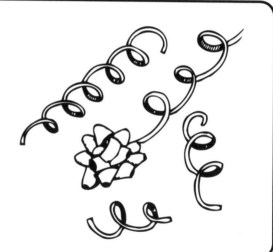

Patriotic Handprints

Start with a piece of **white construction paper**. Dip one hand in **red paint** and press onto paper. Dip the other hand into **blue paint**, and press onto paper. Clean hands with **baby wipes**. When the handprints dry, list patriotic things you do on each finger. Decorate with **glitter** and stars and cut out.

For the Teacher

Set up a handprint station—a desk or table covered with newspaper and stocked with baby wipes. Display the handprints and discuss patriotism.

The Great Seal of the United States

The government adopted the Great Seal of the United States on June 20, 1782. It is used to authenticate important documents. The seal features an eagle, symbolizing self-reliance. It holds an olive branch with 13 leaves and 13 olives in its right talon, and 13 arrows in its left, symbolizing a country that desires peace but has the ability to wage war. Thirteen vertical stripes on the eagle's chest come from the flag of 1777. A blue *chief* (upper section of a shield) above the stripes symbolizes the branches of government.

In the eagle's beak is a scroll inscribed with the motto E Pluribus Unum (ee PLOO-rih-bus YOO-num), a Latin phrase meaning "one out of many," referring to the creation of one nation from 13 states. Benjamin Franklin, John Adams, and Thomas Jefferson, members of the seal committee, suggested the motto. Since 1873, law requires that this motto appear on one side of every United States coin minted.

Project
Create your own great seal.

Materials
- plain white paper
- pencil
- crayons

Directions
1. Sketch out what your "Great Seal" would look like. Be sure to include symbols to represent you and the things that are important to you. Don't forget to include your name!
2. Once your seal is sketched out, color your seal. Use your favorite colors!
3. When everyone is done, go around the room and explain what your seal represents. Post your seals around the classroom or on the classroom door.

    EP075 American Patriotic Symbols © Lab Safety Supply Inc. 2007

Uncle Sam

The term "Uncle Sam" started as a hostile nickname for the United States government during the War of 1812. The term seems to have come about from the large initials *U.S.*, that Samuel Wilson, an army meat inspector, stamped on barrels of salted meat. The nickname was used by people who were opposed to the war, and it spread rapidly.

Uncle Sam's distinct costume, trimmed with stars and stripes, first appeared in the cartoons of the 1830s. His image appeared on many patriotic posters urging men to enlist in the military during World War I. It was used again to urge men and women to work in defense plants during World War II. In 1961, Congress declared that Uncle Sam be recognized as a national symbol.

For the Teacher

Project
Compare WWII era figures and posters.

Materials
Copies or transparencies of WWII era posters (e.g., "I Want You," "We Can Do It," "Buy War Bonds," etc.)

Directions
1. Before class, find copies of WWII posters. Make transparencies for easier viewing by students.
2. Show posters to the students. As a class, make a Compare-and-Contrast chart showing how the posters are similar as well as how they are different.
3. Discuss with students why many WWII posters encouraged people to get involved in the war effort, to conserve materials, and to support their country. Ask them to find and identify other symbols in the posters.

Bald Eagle

The eagle is a fierce, powerful bird that has long been viewed as a symbol of freedom. The United States chose the bald eagle, found only in North America, as its national bird in 1782. The species has been protected by federal law in the continental United States since 1940, and in Alaska since 1953.

A bald eagle may measure 30 to 35 inches (76 to 89 cm) long from its bill to the tip of its tail. It weighs from 8 to 13 pounds (3.6 to 5.9 kg). The long powerful wings have a span of about 7 feet (2.1 m). Bald eagles have strong legs and feet with powerful talons (claws). The beak is well over 1 inch (2.54 cm) long. The bodies of most eagles are dark brown to black. The tail feathers and head feathers are white. A bald eagle builds a nest called an *eyrie*, usually in a tall tree near water. They use the same eyrie every year.

Project
Research symbols of other countries.

Materials
- research materials, Internet access
- white construction paper
- crayons, markers, or colored pencils

Directions
1. Research a national symbol of another country. Find out what this symbol stands for and why the country chose it.

2. Using pencil, make a sketch of the country's symbol. Color with crayons, markers, or colored pencils.

3. Prepare a short presentation to give to the class telling what country you chose, what its symbol is, and the history behind it.

EP075 American Patriotic Symbols © Lab Safety Supply Inc. 2007

Commemorative Stamps

A simple postage stamp has the ability to fan the flames of patriotism by focusing on a country's great leaders and accomplishments. The first stamps issued by the U.S. Post Office appeared in 1847 and bore the portraits of George Washington and Benjamin Franklin, the first U.S. president and postmaster general.

A country may also choose to honor an important event or famous person by issuing a commemorative stamp. The first commemorative stamp issued in the United States was in 1893. It honored the 400th anniversary of the discovery of America and was called the Columbian issue. A stirring patriotic moment captured on a commemorative stamp was the first landing of a man on the moon, issued in 1969.

Project

Work in small groups to create an original, poster-sized commemorative stamp to display on a patriotic bulletin board.

Materials

- magazines and newspapers
- poster board
- crayons
- scissors

Directions

1. Look through magazines and newspapers for information about events and people that stir patriotic feelings. Brainstorm some ideas as a class.

2. Divide into groups of two or three.

3. Select an event or person to commemorate in a stamp.

4. Work together to sketch and color an oversized stamp on poster board to feature on a patriotic bulletin board.

5. Cut the edges of the poster board in a wavy pattern to resemble a postage stamp.

6. Share the story behind your choice for a commemorative stamp.

Star-Spangled Banner

"Star-Spangled Banner" was officially made the U.S. national anthem by Congress in March of 1931. Played at public gatherings and ceremonies, the words were written by Francis Scott Key, and the music was composed by John Stafford Smith.

Key was a Washington D.C. lawyer sent to negotiate the release of a prisoner taken during the War of 1812. As he boarded the British warship, a bombardment of American Fort McHenry began. Key feared for the safety of those inside, but at daybreak he saw the American flag still flying over the fort. He expressed his excitement in a poem penned, for the most part, in just a few minutes. It was distributed on handbills the next morning and quickly became popular.

Other patriotic songs include "Battle Hymn of the Republic," "Dixie," "God Bless America," "America the Beautiful," and "Yankee Doodle." "Hail to the Chief" is an instrumental piece frequently played to honor the president of the United States.

For the Teacher

Project

Illustrate the lyrics from patriotic songs in a painting. Identify and learn to sing the patriotic songs from which the lyrics came.

Materials

- white construction or drawing paper
- watercolor paint or crayons
- Song Lyrics (page 17)

Directions

1. Photocopy the Song lyrics page and cut it apart on the dotted lines. Give a section to each student participating in the project.

2. Encourage students to visualize the lyrics and interpret them in a watercolor painting. Have each student write their lyrics on the bottom of their painting.

3. On a bulletin board decorated with red, white, and blue music notes, post pictures along with the full lyrics to the following six songs: "America," "America the Beautiful," "Star Spangled Banner," "This Land is Your Land," "Yankee Doodle," and "You're a Grand Old Flag."

EP075 American Patriotic Symbols © Lab Safety Supply Inc. 2007

Song Lyrics

 You're a grand old flag,
You're a high flying flag.

 O beautiful, for spacious skies,
For amber waves of grain.

 For purple mountains majesty,
Above the fruited plains.

 Every heart beats true
For the red, white, and blue.

 From every mountainside,
Let freedom ring.

 Crown thy good with brotherhood,
From sea to shining sea.

 And the rockets' red glare,
The bombs bursting in air,
Gave proof thro' the night that our flag
was still there.

 From the mountains,
To the prairies,
To the oceans, white with foam.

 My country 'tis of Thee,
Sweet Land of Liberty
Of Thee I sing.

 As I was walking,
That ribbon of highway,
I saw above me that endless skyway.

 I saw below me,
That golden valley,
This land was made for you and me.

 From the redwood forests,
To the gulf stream waters.
This land was made for you and me.

 Oh! say, can you see,
By the dawn's early light?

 You're the emblem of the land
I love,
The home of the free and the brave.

 Yankee Doodle came to town
A-riding on a pony.

 O beautiful for pilgrim feet
Whose stern, impassioned stress

 Stuck a feather in his cap
And called it macaroni.

 I love thy rocks and rills,
Thy woods and templed hills.

 Thine alabaster cities gleam
Undimmed by human tears.

 O beautiful for patriot dream
That sees beyond the years.

Election Campaign

In 1789, the Electoral College, a group of men chosen by the states, unanimously chose George Washington to serve as our nation's first president. The right to vote and participate in government is the fundamental principal upon which the United States was founded. There are thousands of elections for Congress, state legislatures, city councils, and school boards held every year.

The center of an election is campaign headquarters. Here, volunteers develop and distribute leaflets, prepare mailings, prepare press releases, and perform many other tasks in an effort to get a candidate elected. Campaign headquarters are filled with posters, brochures, and campaign buttons.

On election day, voters receive a ballot from an election clerk, vote secretly, then deposit the ballot in a ballot box.

For the Teacher

Project

Convert a portion of the classroom into an area for completing projects one might find in a campaign headquarters.

Materials

- Campaign Projects
- individual project materials in bold type on page 19

Directions

1. Set up a work table in the classroom. Decorate it with bunting (see page 7).
2. Laminate and post Campaign Projects (page 19) for students to review.
3. Invite students to complete one or more projects. Display the posters on the classroom walls and door, and wear the buttons.

Campaign Projects

Campaign Leaflets

Fold **white writing paper** into three sections. In each section, use **crayons** to draw pictures, create designs, and write inspirational patriotic words that will encourage people to "Get Out and Vote!"

Campaign Posters

Use a **large sheet of white construction paper** and **markers** to create a campaign poster that encourages people to be proud Americans and good citizens. Be sure the poster contains a campaign slogan and patriotic images!

Candidate Campaign Buttons

Cut **white tag board** into 3-inch (7.6 cm) diameter circles. Use this as a pattern to cut the same size circles out of **cardboard**. Use **markers** to write your name and color the tag board circle with patriotic colors and symbols. Put a piece of **double-sided tape** on the back of the button and wear it proudly.

The President of the United States

As chief executive officer and ceremonial head of the government, the president of the United States conducts many ceremonial affairs, makes sure that federal laws are enforced, is responsible for national defense, directs U.S. foreign policy, and makes legislative proposals. The person holding this office should represent the highest American patriotic values and ideals.

As of 2001, the president's salary is $400,000 a year, with an annual expense allowance and maintenance budget for the White House. The president never has a day off and travels with a staff of speech writers, researchers, secretaries, policy advisers, and Secret Service agents.

Incoming White House mail averages thousands of pieces a day. It is read, summarized, and answered by staff members who report to the president.

For the Teacher

Project
Write a letter to the president.

Materials
- Stationery Template
- pencil or pen
- crayons or colored pencils

Directions
1. Reproduce the Stationery Template (page 21) for each student.
2. Brainstorm and discuss places, people, and events that make students feel patriotic and proud to be an American.
3. Have them express these sentiments in a short letter.
4. Have them turn the paper over and illustrate the contents of the letter.
5. Gather the letters and send them in a large envelope to the White House. Have students decorate the envelope with stars and stripes to gain attention. Perhaps you'll get a response!

EP075 American Patriotic Symbols © Lab Safety Supply Inc. 2007

The President of the United States
The White House
1600 Pennsylvania Avenue
Washington, D.C. 20500

Dear Mr. President,

I am proud to be an American because _____

_____

_____

_____

_____

_____

_____

_____

_____

                                        Sincerely,

                                        Age: _____
                                        School: _____

P.S. If you turn the paper over you will find a picture I drew for you of
something that makes me feel especially proud and patriotic!

Washington and Lincoln

George Washington is sometimes called the "Father of His Country." No single person was more instrumental than he in the founding of the United States of America. For 20 years he guided a growing nation. As a military commander, Washington led the Continental Army in its fight for freedom during the Revolutionary War. As president of the convention that wrote the United States Constitution, he helped shape a democratic government. As a political leader he was the first man ever elected president of the United States in 1789.

Abraham Lincoln was the sixteenth president of the United States. He served his country during the turbulent years of the Civil War, from 1861 until his assassination in 1865. Born in Kentucky in 1809, Lincoln rose from humble origins to the nation's highest office. His firm stand against slavery and his determination to preserve the Union symbolize the belief that democracy offers all people a chance to pursue their dreams.

Project

Create mobiles that feature symbols representing two United States presidents.

Materials

- U.S. Map Pattern
- Washington and Lincoln Mobile pages
- red, white, and blue yarn
- red, white, or blue poster board
- scissors
- crayons
- hole punch

Directions

1. Color and cut out the pictures.
2. Punch a hole at the top of each picture.
3. Cut strips of yarn, one for each picture.
4. Cut out and trace the U.S. Map Pattern on tag board. Cut around the outline. Punch a hole at the bottom of the map for each picture.
5. Thread the yarn through the hole at the top of each picture. Tie the other end of the yarn through a hole in the map.

For the Teacher

1. Reproduce the U.S. Map Pattern (page 23) and the Washington and Lincoln Mobile (pages 24–25). Give one to each student, depending on the president he or she has chosen to represent in the mobile.

EP075 American Patriotic Symbols © Lab Safety Supply Inc. 2007

U.S. Map Pattern

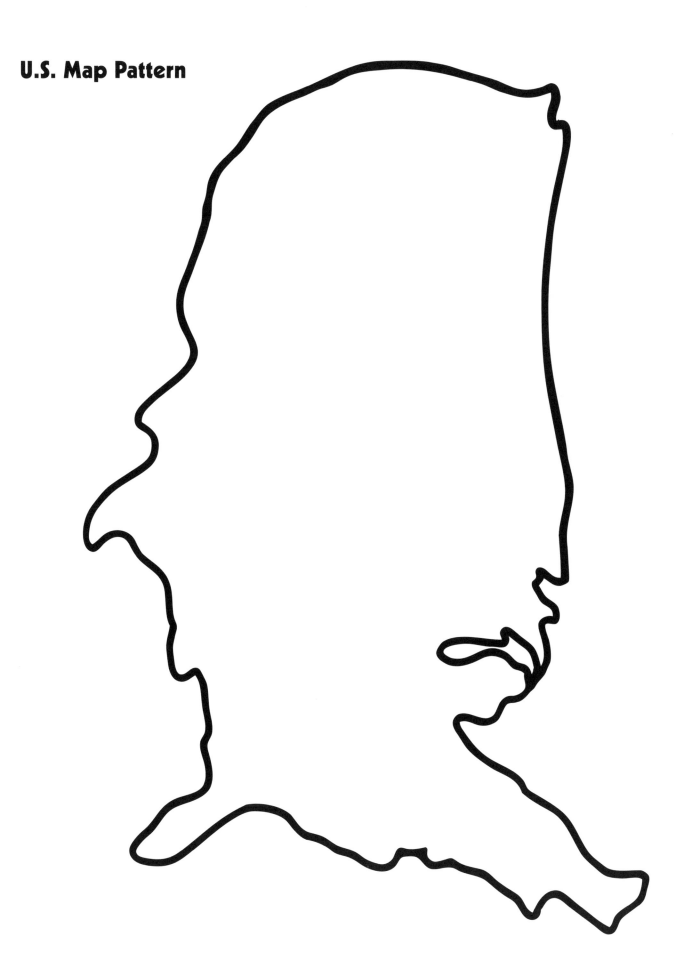

Washington Mobile

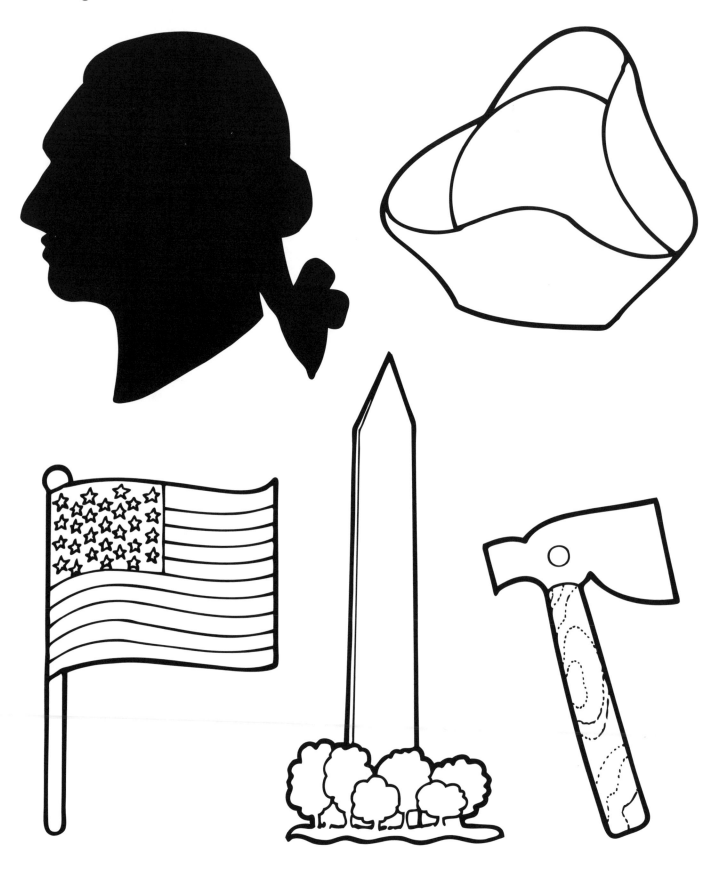

EP075 American Patriotic Symbols © Lab Safety Supply Inc. 2007

Lincoln Mobile

The White House

The White House in Washington, D.C., is the official residence and workplace of the president of the United States. The original construction began in 1792. President and Mrs. John Adams became the first occupants. Renovations and additions have continued since that time, including a rebuilding after being burned by British forces during the War of 1812. It was first called the "President's House" and then the "Executive Mansion." President Theodore Roosevelt authorized "White House" as the official title in 1901.

The house has 132 rooms and stands in the middle of an 18-acre plot. The ground floor includes formal reception areas, the kitchen, and the library. The second floor contains the private living quarters of the president and family. The third floor offers rooms for guests, staff, and storage.

Project

Work with a partner to construct dioramas depicting different rooms in the White House.

Materials

- reference books about the White House
- White House Rooms cards
- shoeboxes
- tempera paint in various colors
- materials gathered by students
- magazines
- paintbrushes
- scissors
- glue

Directions

1. Create shoebox dioramas based on the descriptions on the room cards, plus information gathered from reference books.
2. Share with other students what was learned about the different rooms in the White House.

For the Teacher

1. Divide students into pairs.
2. Copy one set of White House Rooms cards (page 27) for each pair of students.

EP075 American Patriotic Symbols © Lab Safety Supply Inc. 2007

White House Rooms

The Oval Office

The oval office is where the president receives his official visitors. Glass doors lead to the rose garden.

An American flag stands to the right of a large desk, the president's flag to the left. The Great Seal is molded into the ceiling and is woven into the carpet.

One wall contains a marble fireplace. Armchairs are placed in front of it.

The Blue Room

The Blue Room is an oval-shaped reception room where the president receives many of his guests.

A large blue rug bordered with a gold pattern covers the floor.

A large chandelier with tall lights resembling candles hangs from the ceiling.

The State Dining Room

This huge dining room can seat up to 140 dinner guests at one time. It is decorated in gold and white.

The marble fireplace mantel is carved with buffalo heads. Over the fireplace hangs a portrait of Abraham Lincoln.

Sometimes the table is decorated with mirrors and gilded figurines.

The Red Room

The Red Room is a parlor furnished with chairs and couches covered with red fabric.

The walls are covered in red silk fabric edged with gold trim.

A large chandelier with tall lights resembling candles hangs from the ceiling.

A fireplace with a white mantle is centered on one wall.

The Green Room

The Green Room is a parlor filled with couches and chairs covered in shades of green.

A crystal chandelier hangs from the ceiling.

White and green drapes with gold trim and a large gold eagle at the top cover each window.

The floor is covered with a rug in shades of red, pink, and green.

The Library

The library is pale yellow. Its walls are lined with shelves holding several thousand books by American authors.

From the ceiling hangs a crystal chandelier from the home of James Fenimore Cooper.

On the walls are five portraits of American Plains Indians.

The China Room

The China Room was set aside by Mrs. Woodrow Wilson to display samples of the presidential state and family dinner services. The collection was started by Mrs. Benjamin Harrison and is kept in glass cases along the walls.

A full-length portrait of Mrs. Calvin Coolidge hangs in the room.

The Lincoln Bedroom

This bedroom was actually Lincoln's office and cabinet room. It is decorated with a rosewood bed and a table and chairs that were bought while Lincoln lived in the White House.

Many souvenirs of Lincoln's life are here, including his rocking chair, his books, and a copy of the Gettysburg Address.

Capitol Building

The Capitol stands on "Capitol Hill" near the center of Washington, D.C. It is here that Congress meets and carries out the functions of government. The building, constructed in the classical style of ancient Rome, consists of two wings with a huge cast-iron dome on the central section. On top of the dome stands the Statue of Freedom, the figure of a woman wearing a helmet decorated with stars and an eagle's head. In her right hand she holds a shield and laurel wreath; in her left hand, she holds a sheathed sword. The Great Rotunda, which forms the center of the Capitol, consists of the circular area under the dome. The bodies of a number of prominent American citizens have lain in state for viewing.

The Capitol has 540 rooms, including visitors' galleries, offices, and reception rooms. Many rooms feature mementos and paintings of the American past. There is also a President's Room, richly furnished with a huge gold-plated chandelier and portraits of American political leaders.

Project

Paint a historic mural similar to those found in the Capitol building.

Materials

- white butcher paper
- tempera paint
- paintbrushes
- U.S. history reference and picture books

Directions

1. Look through picture and reference books, then brainstorm a list of famous and memorable events in U.S. history.

2. Divide into cooperative groups. Each group should select an event to depict in a mural.

3. Sketch the illustration and then paint the mural. Post murals in the classroom.

EP075 American Patriotic Symbols © Lab Safety Supply Inc. 2007

The Washington Monument

A gleaming white marble obelisk, rising 555 feet (169.2 m) into the air, graces the Washington, D.C., landscape. It is situated halfway between the Lincoln Memorial and the Capitol building in a park-like setting near the Potomac River. Built in honor of the first president of the United States, it is known as the Washington Monument.

Originally planned while George Washington was still living, the plans were scrapped because he did not approve of the expense. Nevertheless, a group of people began raising funds for the project in 1833. The same trowel used by Washington to lay the Capitol building cornerstone in 1783 was again used to lay the original monument cornerstone on July 4, 1848. However, engineers determined the ground to be too soft to support the structure, so a new site was selected and the building process began again.

Project #1

Make a stand-up model of the Washington Monument.

Materials

- two large sheets white construction paper
- scissors
- pencil
- ruler
- glue

Directions

1. Fold each sheet of construction paper in half lengthwise.

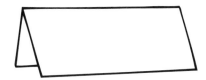

2. Measure 2 inches (5 cm) from the fold at one end of the paper. Make a mark. Measure 5 inches (12.7 cm) from the fold at the other end, and make a mark. Draw a straight line between the marks, then cut on the line. Repeat the steps on a second piece of construction paper.

3. Fold in ½ inch (1.27 cm) on each length of the

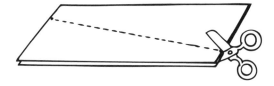

construction paper to create a flap. Overlap the flaps and glue them together, connecting all four sides to create a dimensional model.

Project #2

Research national monuments.

Materials

- research materials

Directions

1. Choose a national monument to research. Find out when and why it was built, who it honors, and its significance today.

2. Draw a picture of your monument and color.

3. Report your findings to the class.

The Statue of Liberty

The Statue of Liberty, a gift from France to the United States in 1884, is a symbol of American democracy and a symbol of refuge for immigrants. The French people donated about $250,000 for its construction. The statue was shipped in 214 cases and reassembled on Bedloe's Island overlooking New York Harbor. President Grover Cleveland dedicated the monument in 1886.

The statue is an example of repoussé art. This process involves the hammering of metal over a mold in order to shape it. More than 300 thin sheets of copper weighing about 100 short tons (90.7 metric tons) were used to fashion the statue. Liberty measures more than 305 feet (93 m) from the sandals to the tip of her torch. Two parallel stairways, each with 168 steps, spiral inside the statue from the base to the crown. The crown has an observation platform with 25 windows that accommodates as many as 30 viewers at any one time. The seven rays in Liberty's crown stand for the seven continents of the world.

Project
Create a paper crown similar to that worn by "Liberty." Memorize lines from a poem inscribed on the statue.

For the Teacher
Copy one Liberty's Crown Pattern (page 31) per student.

Materials
- Liberty's Crown Pattern
- large sheet white construction paper
- aluminum foil
- tape
- gold spray paint or yellow tempera paint
- scissors
- pencil
- paintbrush

Directions
1. Cut out the pattern.
2. Trace the pattern twice onto a large sheet of construction paper. Cut out and tape the two pieces together to form a circle.
3. Cover the crown with aluminum foil pressed into shape.
4. Spray with gold paint or brush with yellow tempera paint to create a copper effect.
5. Learn several well-known lines from a poem inscribed on the tablet in the statue's pedestal to recite while wearing the crown.

"… Give me your tired, your poor,
Your huddled masses yearning to breathe free,
The wretched refuse of your teeming shore.
Send these, the homeless, tempest-tossed to me,
I lift my lamp beside the golden door!"

Liberty's Crown Pattern

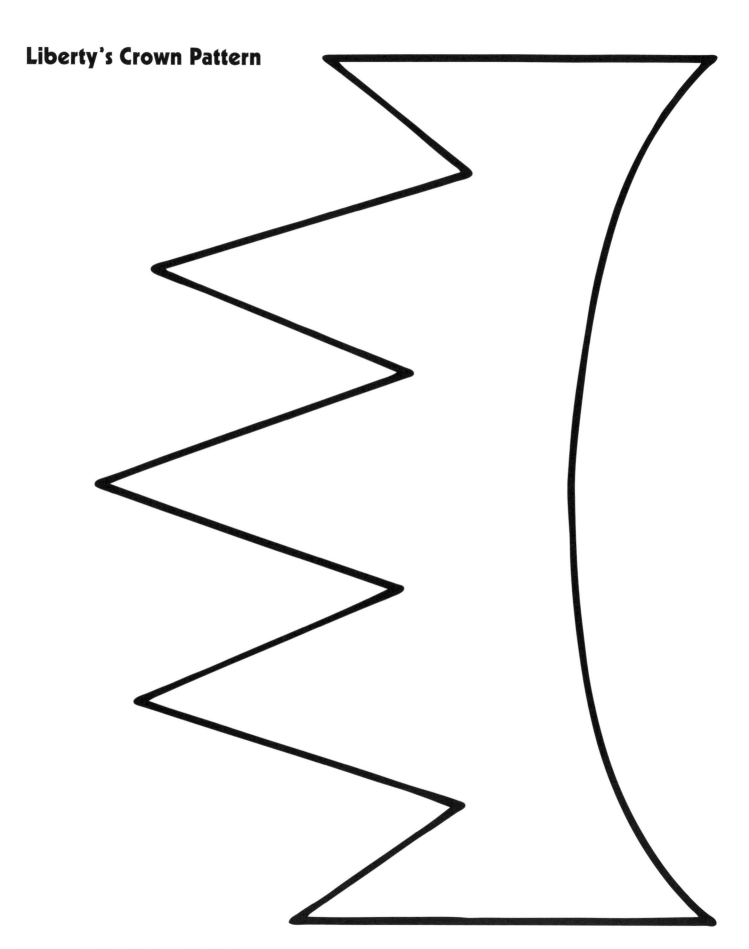

The Liberty Bell

The Liberty Bell, weighing more than 2,080 pounds (943 kg), is one of the earliest symbols of American freedom. Its inscription, "Proclaim Liberty throughout all the land unto all the inhabitants thereof," is from the Bible (Leviticus 25:10). In 1752, the province of Pennsylvania paid about $300 for it. After its arrival from England, where it was originally cast, it cracked while ringing. It was recast in Philadelphia, using the same metal and inscription. It was rung with other church bells on July 8, 1776, to announce the adoption of the Declaration of Independence, and on each anniversary thereafter. The bell broke again in 1835 while being rung during the funeral of John Marshall, Chief Justice of the United States.

The Liberty Bell is no longer rung, although it has been struck from time to time. One such occasion was June 6, 1944, when Allied forces landed in France.

Project
Make a small model of the Liberty Bell.

Materials
- small plastic bleach (or similar-shaped) bottle with no handle
- scissors
- sponges
- masking tape
- brown and yellow tempera paint
- thin-tipped black marker

Directions
1. Cut about 3 inches (7.6 cm) off the bottom of the bottle. Cut a narrow opening about 2 inches (5 cm) long up from the bottom edge, to create the crack in the bell.

2. Cut masking tape into short lengths and cover the entire surface of the bottle. Add extra layers of tape to the bottom edges to create a curved, bell shape. Write the Liberty Bell's inscription on a longer strip of masking tape and place it around the upper part of the bottle.

3. Mix the tempera paint to create a bronze shade. Sponge-paint to cover the tape.

EP075 American Patriotic Symbols © Lab Safety Supply Inc. 2007

Mount Rushmore

Mount Rushmore, a giant sculpture carved into the side of a mountain, is located in the Black Hills of South Dakota. It was started in 1927 to symbolize American growth and leaders. Each of the faces on the mountain is 60 feet (18.3 m) tall. Almost three million people from around the world visit Mount Rushmore each year.

The four presidents carved into Mount Rushmore are George Washington, Thomas Jefferson, Theodore Roosevelt, and Abraham Lincoln. These presidents were chosen because they symbolize struggles that the American people have gone through that have defined American history. George Washington symbolizes the struggle for independence from Great Britain. Thomas Jefferson represents the Declaration of Independence, which he wrote, and the 1803 Louisiana Purchase, which doubled the size of the United States. Theodore Roosevelt symbolizes the economic growth of the twentieth century, and the United States' role in world events. Abraham Lincoln signifies the preservation of the union and the struggle against slavery.

Project

Do research to choose four people to make up your own Mount Rushmore.

Materials

- paper
- pencil
- markers, colored pencils, or crayons
- encyclopedias and/or Internet access

Directions

1. Think of historical figures and presidents who you think represent American ideals.

2. Choose four presidents or other historical figures who are not on Mount Rushmore. Use encyclopedias and the Internet to research these people. Take notes on what made them memorable, good things that they did, what they stood for, etc.

3. Draw and color a picture of each of your presidents or figures, and then write a paragraph describing why you think he or she should be on Mount Rushmore.

4. Present your "New Mount Rushmore" to the class and explain why you chose each person.

Medals

George Washington created the first U.S. military medal (decoration), the *Badge of Military Merit*, in 1782, to honor his soldiers for bravery during the Revolutionary War. This medal eventually became known as the Purple Heart. Other U.S. military medals include the *Medal of Honor*, the *Silver Star*, and the *Bronze Star*. Civilians can earn the *Presidential Medal of Freedom* for cultural or public services. The *Young American Medals* for Bravery and for Service are awarded to boys or girls under the age of 19.

Persons who receive decorations must meet certain standards. The majority of the decorations are in the shape of a cross or star; others are round. They are made of silver or bronze and hang from a pin or from ribbons of varying color combinations. Each medal bears its own design and motto.

Project

Use a variety of craft materials to design a medal to award to classroom citizens for outstanding behavior or kind deeds.

Materials

- assorted art materials including cardboard, aluminum foil, ribbon, buttons, pin backs, gift wrap, construction paper, raffia, stickers, costume jewelry, yarn
- scissors
- stapler
- tacky glue
- safety pins

Directions

1. Sketch an original design for a medal.
2. Select the art medium for the medal and carry out the design. Hang with ribbon or use tacky glue to add a pin back.
3. Explain the type of person to whom, or the circumstances for which, the medal should be awarded. Select a classmate who has met the criteria and present the medal.

EP075 American Patriotic Symbols © Lab Safety Supply Inc. 2007

Fireworks

The colorful sparks and loud noises created by exploding fireworks are often associated with patriotic events and parades. Independence Day (Fourth of July) celebrations are usually capped by a display of fireworks, oftentimes accompanied by patriotic music.

However, most fireworks, also called pyrotechnics, can be dangerous because they are made by packing gunpowder into hollow paper tubes. Manufacturers add small amounts of special chemicals to the gunpowder to create colors. Most states prohibit the use of fireworks by individuals. The federal government also limits the explosive power that can be used by individuals. Many safety precautions must be taken by companies that conduct fireworks displays for audiences to enjoy.

Project

Create a Fourth of July fireworks hat.

Materials

- red, white, and blue construction paper
- scissors
- gold or silver pipe cleaners
- glue and tape
- sparkly craft balls or star stickers

Directions

1. Cut two 3-inch-high strips of blue construction paper. Glue one end together and measure around head. Leave 2 inches extra and cut excess. Do not glue ends.

2. Cut red and white construction paper into 2½ x 12-inch strips. Lay the strips next to each other in alternating colors. Place glue on top along the blue strip and lay it on the strips of white and red construction paper.

3. Turn the headband over and place a sparkly pipe cleaner every 3 inches along the headband. Use tape to hold in place. Add sparkly craft balls or place star stickers back to back on the top of each pipe cleaner.

4. Wrap hat around head and secure with a large paper clip or fit to head and glue. Allow to dry.

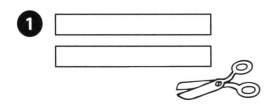

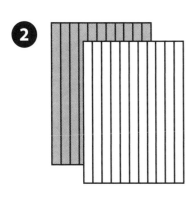

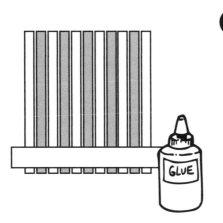

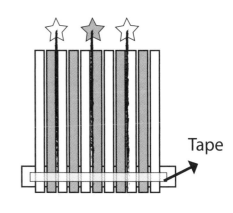

Tape

National Holidays

Many national holidays are patriotic. The president and Congress select those to be observed in Washington, D.C., and by federal employees. Congress has also, on occasion, set aside special days to celebrate historic events such as V-J Day, which commemorates the end of fighting in World War II. Some states observe Election Day (the first Tuesday after the first Monday in November) in the year of a presidential election. The governor of each state has the authority to specify the holidays a particular state will observe.

It is customary for banks and schools to be closed on national holidays. If a holiday falls on a Saturday or Sunday, it is generally celebrated the following Monday.

For the Teacher

Project

Work in cooperative groups to create projects for a tabletop display featuring a national holiday or celebration.

Materials

- Holiday Project Page (page 37)
- assorted materials based on the project selected by each group

Directions

1. Divide into eight cooperative groups. Cut apart the holiday project cards. Give one to each group.

2. Have each group assemble the materials needed to complete the projects on their project card and gather further information about the holiday or celebration they've been assigned.

3. Arrange the completed projects in a tabletop exhibit to be shared with classmates. Invite other classrooms to visit and learn more about patriotic holidays.

EP075 American Patriotic Symbols © Lab Safety Supply Inc. 2007

Holiday Project Page

Martin Luther King Jr.'s Birthday

January 15

- Draw a picture of a dream or wish you have.
- Learn to sing a "spiritual."
- Write an acrostic poem about equality using King's name.
- Make a banner featuring the word EQUALITY.

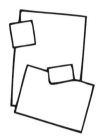

Presidents' Day

Third Monday in February

- Create a rolled-paper log cabin.
- Make a poster board top hat.
- Use tissue paper and starch to create a cherry tree.
- Fashion a three-cornered hat from construction paper.

Flag Day

June 14

- Cover the classroom door to look like a flag.
- Use cloth scraps to make a red, white, and blue wall hanging.
- Decorate a star for each state.
- Color white stars by painting blue watercolor over them.

Citizenship Day

September 17

- Design patriotic stationery.
- Make a "Good Citizen" award.
- Clip newspaper articles about good citizenship and create a collage.
- Design a quilt square using red, white, and blue.

Independence Day

July 4

- Bake a birthday cake for your country.
- Paint a "firecracker-sky" mural.
- Cut and paste magazine letters to create firecracker words like pop, boom, and crackle.
- Design patriotic giftwrap.

Memorial Day

The last Monday in May

- Use family photos to create a "memory" collage.
- Invite a veteran to share a special story on tape.
- Make a bouquet of red paper poppies.
- Create a model battleship.

Labor Day

The first Monday in September

- Create a shoebox diorama showing someone "on the job."
- Design a paper plate mobile that shows the future job you want.
- Make a paperweight to give to someone who has a "desk job."
- Make a magazine-picture poster of people at work.

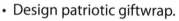

Veterans Day

November 11

- Create a banner that features the word PEACE.
- Listen to military marches.
- Demonstrate a salute used by someone in the military.
- Use ribbon and stickers to make a medal.

Parades

Everyone loves a parade! At least that's the way it seems in the United States! During the 1880s and 1890s, people in the U.S. found political parades to be extremely popular. The U.S. armed forces often paraded on holidays. This was a way of reminding citizens of their country's military strength and skill.

Parades have evolved into community events honoring a particular occasion or federal holiday. They feature civic groups, government leaders, youth groups, bands, floats, banners, and flags. When a national flag is carried in a parade with other flags, it should always be on the marching right. On a float, a national flag should be hung from a staff with its folds falling free, or it should be hung flat.

For the Teacher

Project

Plan and carry out a patriotic parade.

Materials

- Parade Activities
- see individual activities for materials

Directions

1. Copy one Parade Activities (page 39) per student.

2. As a class, plan the parade. Record all ideas on chart paper. Make final choices, then break down the plans into smaller, cooperative group tasks. Divide the class into groups and assign each group a duty, or allow students to sign up for the work group they would prefer.

3. Create a list showing the order of the parade. On the day of the parade, have students dress in patriotic colors and play patriotic music.

Parade Activities

Plan a Parade Route

- Plan a parade route.
- Create a map that shows the route.
- Make copies to send to all your guests. Indicate on the map where people should sit. Assign class members to be in charge of "crowd control" during the parade.

Paint Parade Banners

- Create banners to carry in the parade.
- Cut a piece of butcher paper. Paint patriotic symbols or slogans on it. Wrap one length around a long PVC pipe.
- Tape in place. Place a person at each end to carry the banner in the parade.

Design a Float

- Assign several groups to design floats.
- The floats may be created on wagons, boxes pulled by bicycles, or other imaginative transportation.
- Decorate them with streamers, crepe paper, or butcher paper.
- Be sure they represent the parade's theme!

Be a Color Guard

- Learn to be color guard and proudly march with the American flag in the parade.
- Non-military color guards include one color-bearer and two escorts.
- When a flag passes by, the audience should stand to salute it.

All-American Food

The food and cooking styles in America are as diverse as its people. Regional and ethnic dishes abound, while picnics and outdoor barbecues are popular holiday pastimes.

You've probably heard the saying: "As American as apple pie." Apples have been a favorite fruit of people since the Stone Age, and this fruit has been important as an American crop. Early American colonists brought apple seeds and apples from England. As settlers moved westward across America, they took apples and seedling trees with them. John Chapman, a pioneer and apple planter, distributed apple sprouts to settlers in northern and central Ohio. The legend of Johnny Appleseed, as Chapman became known, grew during the 1800s and became synonymous with the pioneering spirit of America. The "fruited plains" of the midwest also provided the imagery for the song lyrics of one of our most popular patriotic songs, "America the Beautiful."

Project

Cook in the classroom and prepare some food with patriotic flavor!

For the Teacher

Copy one set of All-American Food Recipes (pages 40–41) per student.

Materials

- bowls, baking pans, spoons, spatulas, measuring cups and spoons, plastic knives
- All-American Food recipes
- additional utensils as per recipe
- recipe ingredients

Red, White, & Blueberries

Ingredients

- strawberries
- blueberries
- frozen whipped topping, thawed (plain yogurt may be substituted)

Directions

1. Wash and pat dry all the fruit.
2. Slice strawberries.
3. Layer ingredients in a clear plastic cup: strawberries on the bottom, topping in the middle, blueberries on top.

All-American Food Recipes

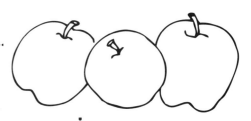

Apple Pizza Pie

Ingredients

- 1 cup (240 ml) biscuit mix
- ¼ cup (60 ml) water
- 1 cup (240 ml) applesauce
- ½ tsp. (2.5 ml) cinnamon
- 1/8 tsp. (.6 ml) nutmeg
- 6 Tbsp. (90 ml) flour
- 1/3 cup (75 ml) sugar
- ¼ cup (60 ml) softened butter

Directions

1. Combine biscuit mix and water. Knead lightly and pat out into a circle on foil.
2. Spread applesauce onto crust.
3. Combine remaining dry ingredients. Cut in the butter. Sprinkle over applesauce.
4. Bake at 425°F (218°C) for 20 to 25 minutes.

Cowboy Beans

Ingredients

- 1 large can of pork and beans, including liquid
- 1 large can whole kernel corn, drained
- 4 hot dogs, sliced
- 1 medium onion, chopped
- 1 Tbsp. (15 ml) butter

Directions

1. Brown hot dogs and onion in butter.
2. Add drained corn and the pork and beans.
3. Cook over medium heat until heated through.

Easy Picnic Sandwiches

Ingredients

- 2 slices bread
- spreadable cream cheese
- strawberry jam

Directions

1. Use star-shaped cookie cutter to shape bread slices.
2. Spread one piece of bread with cream cheese and jam. Top with second piece of bread.

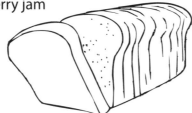

Coloring Pages Projects

Project
Color or paint each of the following pages. Then choose from the ideas to create a patriotic symbol.

Materials
- Coloring Pages
- crayons
- watercolors
- scissors

For the Teacher
Copy the project ideas (below) and one set of Coloring Pages (43–47) for each student.

 ### Stand-up Panel

Create an accordion-fold, stand-up picture panel.

 ### Picture Folder

Staple file folders together in the center. Glue a picture to each page.

3 ### Wall Border

Place the pictures side-by-side to create a patriotic border for the classroom wall.

 ### Mobile

Cut out the pictures. Hang them with yarn from a clothes hanger.

EP075 American Patriotic Symbols © Lab Safety Supply Inc. 2007

Statue of Liberty

Liberty Bell

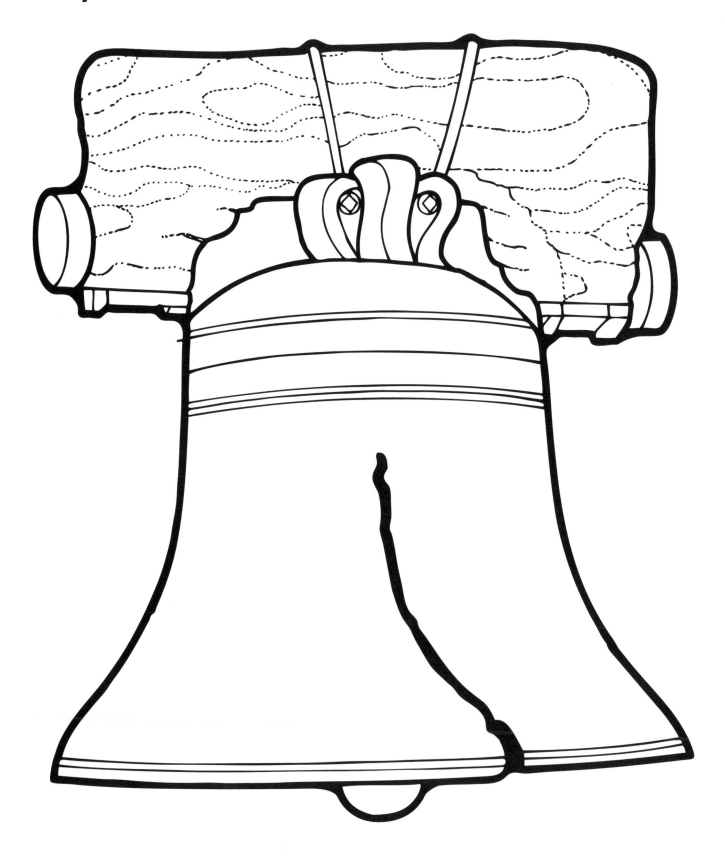

 EP075 American Patriotic Symbols © Lab Safety Supply Inc. 2007

Great Seal of the United States

American Flag

Capitol Dome

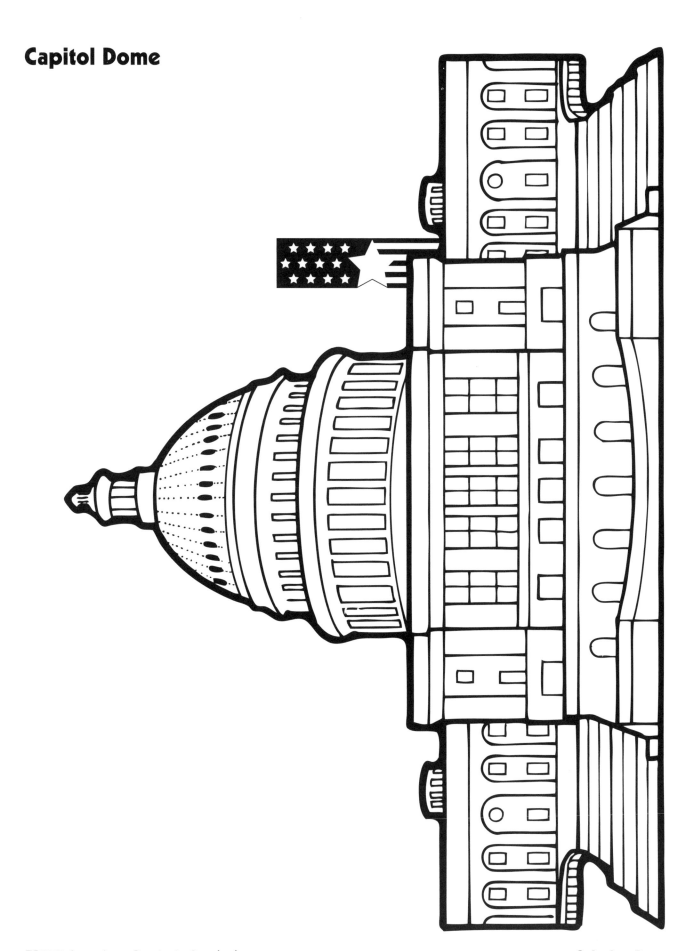

Literature List

America the Beautiful
by Katherine Lee Bates. Little, Brown and Company, 2004. 32 p. Gr. 1–5
Illustrator Chris Gall, the great great grandnephew of Katharine Lee Bates, pays homage to this musical symbol of our country. Includes musical notes and a copy of the song's lyrics written in Bates's hand.

America the Beautiful, a Pop–Up Book
by Robert Sabuda. Little Simon, 2004. 16 p. All ages
Master paper engineer Robert Sabuda interprets the American anthem "America the Beautiful" from the Golden Gate Bridge to Mount Rushmore to the Statue of Liberty.

Capital
by Lynn Curlee. Atheneum, 2003. 48 p. Gr. 3–6
Provides a history of Washington, D.C., focusing on the National Mall, its monuments, and surrounding buildings.

Fireworks, Picnics, and Flags: The Story of the Fourth of July Symbols
by James Cross Giblin. Clarion Books, 2001. 96 p. Gr. 3–6
A lively book that traces the social history behind America's celebration of Independence Day and explains the background of such national symbols as the flag, the bald eagle, the Liberty Bell, and Uncle Sam.

I Pledge Allegiance
by Bill Martin Jr. Candlewick Press, 2002. 40 p. Gr. 1–4
With simple, straightforward language and playfully quirky illustrations by Chris Raschka, a look at each word of the Pledge of Allegiance and what it means.

O, Say Can You See? America's Symbols, Landmarks, and Inspiring Words
by Sheila Keenan. Scholastic, 2004. 64 p. Gr. 1–5
This celebration of 20 of America's important places, interesting objects, and inspiring words is arranged in two-page spreads illustrated in bright pastels.

A Picnic in October
by Eve Bunting. Harcourt, 1999. 32 p. Gr. 1–3
A boy finally comes to understand why his grandmother insists that the family come to Ellis Island each year to celebrate Lady Liberty's birthday.

Red, White, Blue and Uncle Who?
by Teresa Bateman. Holiday House, 2003. 64 p. Gr. 3–6
From the White House to Mount Rushmore, this book explains the origins of 17 patriotic symbols.

Saving the Liberty Bell
by Megan McDonald. Atheneum/Richard Jackson Books, 2005. 32 p. Gr. 1–3
When John Jacob Mickley accompanies his father on a trip to Philadelphia, he discovers that the city is facing a Redcoat attack. Next thing he knows, Papa and he have been entrusted with a top-secret mission. Can the humble Mickley wagon dodge British soldiers and carry an important 2,000-pound symbol of freedom to safety?

Stars and Stripes: The Story of the American Flag
by Sarah L. Thomson. HarperCollins, 2003. 32 p. Gr. 1–4
Visually appealing introduction to the history of the American flag, from colonial times to the present.

The White House: An Illustrated History
by Catherine O. Grace. Scholastic Reference, 2003. 144 p. Gr. 3–8
Explores the history, architecture, and symbolism of the White House, which serves as a museum, office, ceremonial site, and home to presidents and their families.